MAPS TODAY

Gareth Stevens
Publishing

Please visit our Web site www.garethstevens.com. For a free color catalog of all our high-quality books, call toll free 1-800-542-2595 or fax 1-877-542-2596.

Library of Congress Cataloging-in-Publication Data

Maps today / Tim Cooke, editor.

      p. cm. -- (Understanding maps of our world)

    Includes index.

    ISBN 978-1-4339-3521-3 (library binding) -- ISBN 978-1-4339-3522-0 (pbk.)

    ISBN 978-1-4339-3523-7 (6-pack)

    1. Maps--Juvenile literature. 2. Cartography--Juvenile literature. I. Cooke, Tim (Tim A.)

  GA105.6.M4 2010

  912--dc22
                                          2009039222

Published in 2010 by

Gareth Stevens Publishing

111 East 14th Street, Suite 349

New York, NY 10003

© 2010 The Brown Reference Group Ltd.

For Gareth Stevens Publishing:

Art Direction: Haley Harasymiw

Editorial Direction: Kerri O'Donnell

For The Brown Reference Group Ltd:

Editorial Director: Lindsey Lowe

Managing Editor: Tim Cooke

Children's Publisher: Anne O'Daly

Design Manager: David Poole

Designer: Simon Morse

Production Director: Alastair Gourlay

Picture Manager: Sophie Mortimer

Picture Researcher: Clare Newman

Picture Credits:

Front Cover: NASA: Landsat; Shutterstock: Alexandru Olaru Radian: br

Brown Reference Group: all artwork

Corbis: Roger Ressmeyer 36; David Sailors 15; Department of Defense: 37; DigitalVision: 4m, 4b; Jupiter Images: Ablestock 5m; Liquid Library 17; Stockxpert 5t, 32; NASA: 7, 26, 27, 28; Landsat 21, 24, 25, 30, 31, 40; Shutterstock: Giovanni Benintende 41; Steve Estvanik 42; Vladislav Gurfinkel 4t; Morgan Land Photography 16; Alexandru Olaru Radian 39; Rasch 44; Konstantin Shevtsov 19; Sofia 33; Steven Wright 5b

Publisher's note to educators and parents: Our editors have carefully reviewed the Web sites that appear on p. 46 to ensure that they are suitable for students. Many Web sites change frequently, however, and we cannot guarantee that a site's future contents will continue to meet our high standards of quality and educational value. Be advised that students should be closely supervised whenever they access the Internet.

Manufactured in the United States of America

1 2 3 4 5 6 7 8 9 12 11 10

CPSIA compliance information: Batch #BRW0102GS: For further information contact Gareth Stevens, New York, New York at 1-800-542-2595.

Contents

The Changing Shape of the World

This map shows the world known to Europeans in the fifteenth century: Europe and parts of Asia and Africa.

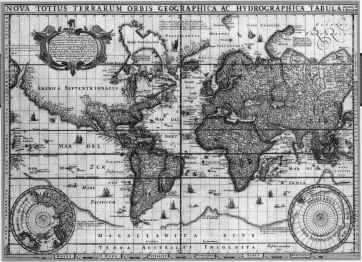

1700

1600

In this seventeenth-century map, only the interior of North America and the southern oceans remain empty.

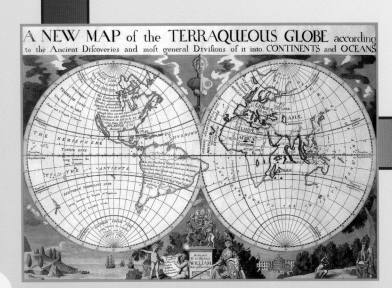

1800

This map reveals more information about Australia, but the northwest coast of North America and most of the Pacific Ocean remain unknown.

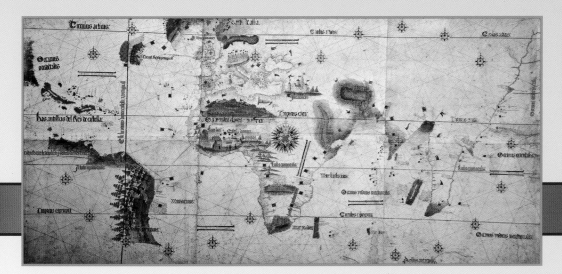

This sixteenth-century map fills in the coasts of Africa and India, the Caribbean islands, and parts of South America.

1500

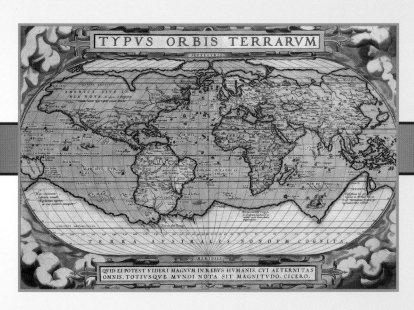

In this sixteenth-century map, South America is only roughly shaped; the northwest coast of Australia has become part of the legendary "southern continent."

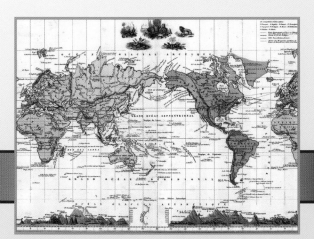

The first photographs of Earth from space were taken only in the 1960s.

1900

This world map was drawn in 1875, when Europeans were at the height of claiming colonies in other lands.

Introduction

This is a volume from the set Understanding Maps of Our World. This book looks at how maps and mapping help travelers find their way.

UNDERSTANDING MAPS OF OUR WORLD IS AN eight-volume set that describes the history of cartography, discusses its importance in different cultures, and explains how it is done. Cartography is the technique of compiling information for, and then drawing, maps or charts. Each volume in the set examines a particular aspect of mapping and uses numerous artworks and photographs to help the reader understand the sometimes complex themes.

After all, cartography is both a science and an art. It has existed since before words were written down and today uses the most up-to-date computer technology and imaging systems. Advances in mapmaking through history have been closely involved with wider advances in science and technology. Studying maps demands some understanding of math and at the same time an appreciation of visual creativity. Such a subject is bound to get a little complex at times!

About This Book

This book examines the way that computer technology has changed the way that maps are created and used. Today, mapmaking is computerized: map coordinates can be combined with other data in geographical information systems (GIS) to create customized maps for many different purposes. These digital maps can include pictures, such as aerial photographs and satellite images. Our maps of the solar system are also continually improving as space probes provide more and better information. Maps no longer have to be printed on paper: the Internet allows maps to be distributed anywhere in the world cheaply and efficiently.

→ **The first photograph of the whole Earth from space, taken by the crew of Apollo 8 in 1968. The lower part of Earth is in shadow. Views of Earth from space are now an important part of mapping.**

Digital Maps

Until the 1970s, almost every map was created by hand. Today almost all maps are computer-generated. This has a number of advantages over the old method.

TODAY PEOPLE WANT MAPS that are suited to their particular needs. For the first time, this is possible. Some people use maps only to check that they are on the right route. Other people want to use a map alongside other information to test a theory. Someone traveling on a bus does not want the same kind of map as a scientist examining climate change.

Preparing a map for printing is expensive. This means that cartographers lose money if they

This map was drawn by hand using pen and ink. For hand-drawn maps to be printed, the draftsman or draftswoman had to prepare a different sheet for each color on the map—in this case the black, yellow, and blue detail. (The green features were drawn on both the blue and yellow sheets and showed green in those overlapping areas in the printed version.)

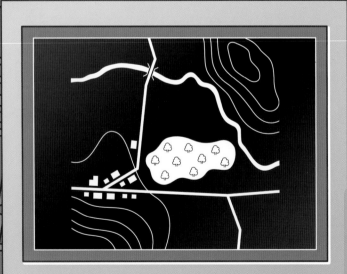

The same data can be displayed in a computer software package. Here the detail has been drawn simply. The information held in the computer is a list of coordinates (positions) of each point or bend in a line or outline of an area. The coordinates are plotted and joined together to create this basic map.

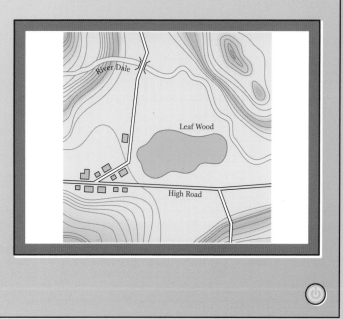

Computer software can help design as well as plot detail. Here the map has been made to look exactly the same as the hand-drawn map on page 8. Text has been added and the design can be easily altered.

print a map that only a small group of people will want to buy. Printed maps are not only expensive to make, but they also become out-of-date quickly.

Maps today can be produced for smaller groups of people. The map can be changed to show different features. The same map can be made to look different by changing the design. Maps can be combined with other information. Maps no longer need to be stored on a shelf; they appear and disappear at the touch of a switch. All this is made possible by digital mapping, the name given to computer-assisted cartography.

Computers and Maps

Maps can be drawn more quickly using a computer than by hand. Also, it is usually cheaper to produce a map using a computer, as you need only a little drawing ability and mistakes can be easily fixed. Using a computer, almost anyone can produce a usable map.

Computer programs process and store information in a different way from people. All the information that you find on a map has to be converted into numbers before a computer program can use or store it. Some information on maps is already recorded in numbers, such as the heights of hills and mountains. Converting information like the route of a road into numbers is more complicated.

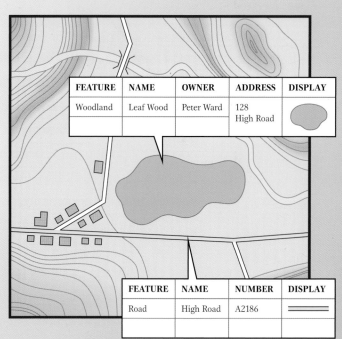

FEATURE	NAME	OWNER	ADDRESS	DISPLAY
Woodland	Leaf Wood	Peter Ward	128 High Road	

FEATURE	NAME	NUMBER	DISPLAY
Road	High Road	A2186	

As well as holding the map coordinates, a computer can also retain an enormous amount of information in its database about the attributes, or properties, of the features shown, such as names, to be called up as needed.

Points, Lines, and Areas in the Computer

The task of converting information about the real world into a form suitable for the computer is called *digitizing*. The positions of features are entered on the computer in the form of coordinates. These coordinates can be recorded as a list of individual points, with each representing an individual feature. They can also be stored as a series of connected points in order to define a line. If the coordinates of the last point in a series of connected points are the same as those of the first point, then the line defines an area.

So, the three main types of features on a map—points, lines, and areas—can be stored in a computer as a set of coordinates. Once they have been entered into a file called a database, we can run a computer program that will draw them onto the computer screen. Such a program is part of a software package that includes computer graphics.

Additional Design Information

If you were to use the computer graphics program to plot a set of coordinates from the database, it is likely that you would see a black screen with some white areas, lines, and points on it. They would be accurately positioned representations of features on Earth's surface, but they would not look like a well-designed map. Additional information is needed to tell the computer how to design the look of the map.

The database with the coordinates can also hold design information, such as "the line shown by these coordinates will be drawn in red" or "the color inside this area is light green." The database can also include the name of a feature, so that the lettering is included on the computer-drawn map automatically.

Digitizing

It would take a long time to manually type in all the coordinates of features in the real world. The largest store of coordinate information comes from maps that have already been produced. Digital mapping relies on databases that have been created by transforming, or digitizing, paper maps. Digitizing from paper maps is a long and tedious operation, but once the information is in the database, it is very useful.

Some Advantages of Digital Maps

In addition to holding the usual map information of point, line, and area (like the maps on pages 8 and 9), digital mapping can capture and manipulate other information.

Here the positions and heights of points on the landscape have been measured and digitized by surveyors in the field. Back in the office the digital mapping software has created a pattern of triangles between the points surveyed. In the map on the right the software has traced contours through the array of points, transforming the map of the landscape relief into a line map. Once this information is available, it can be passed on to the type of geographic information system explained on pages 12–13.

The cartographer can now highlight areas above a certain height by a simple instruction to the computer. Different displays can be prepared. Each of the triangles defines an area of even slope and aspect (direction of slope), so hill shading can be automatically created. The map scale can be changed with a few keystrokes on the computer, as here: the right-hand map is smaller scale.

Imagine that this hilly area is a forest. The foresters want to log all the trees, but their logging machinery can only move across slopes that are not too steep. The computer can calculate which of the triangles of land can be crossed by the machinery and highlight them. With the right software, it can even recommend the most efficient order in which to clear the trees.

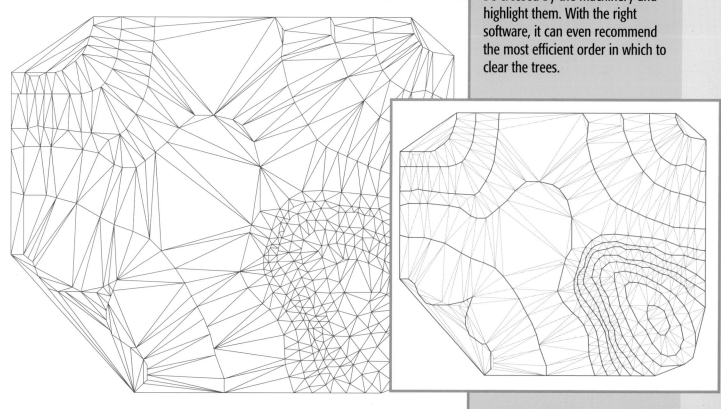

Databases are now able to receive information supplied by a GPS receiver. A series of positions is recorded by the receiver as, for example, the GPS user walks along a road. That series of coordinates is fed directly into the computer, which uses them to add the road to the map in progress. GPS makes it much easier to keep maps up to date.

GIS

Digital mapping is made possible by computer programs called geographical information systems (GIS). These programs allow users to create their own thematic maps.

COMPUTER DATABASES CAN STORE LOTS MORE information than traditionally appears on maps. On a paper map, you could identify a town, and perhaps have enough space to record its name and population. A database allows you to add much more information than you could ever add to a paper map.

For example, the database might also include the names of businesses in the town, and what each one does. It could include the value of the homes on different streets, or the volume of traffic on those streets during rush hour. It could also display details like air and noise pollution levels, the catchment areas of different schools, crime levels, and the average income of the residents.

This is a map drawn from a very large database of information about the city of La Grande, Oregon. The database is the core of the city geographic information system, which can plot maps like this showing a lot of detail of the streets in the city center. This map was produced to show the impact of diesel pollution.

CITY OF LA GRANDE
Diesel Impact Area

Legend

☐ City Limits — Highways

☐ UGB ┅ Railroad

☐ Diesel — Rivers

Properties on the periphery may be only partially impacted; however, entire blocks are highlighted.

Feet
0 200 400 600 800

1" = 350'
11/01/99 01.32 PM

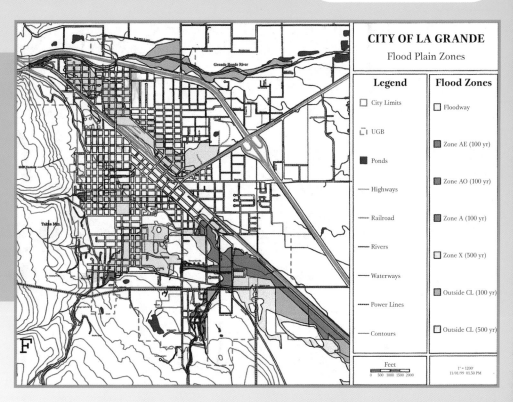

This map was drawn from the same database, but shows less detail in the city center and more in the suburbs. The shape, or relief, of the land is also presented by contour lines. Data has been combined using the GIS to calculate the areas that are most at risk from flooding.

Once all this information has been put into the database, a range of different maps can be generated. For example, a map can show the distribution of shops and businesses in the area, or show which routes become most congested at rush hour. A map that shows the crime levels in different areas of the town would be very useful to a police commander planning patrols.

Using a GIS, it is possible to display different sets of information together on the same map. This allows the user to easily spot patterns or connections between different phenomena. For example, town planners might be interested in comparing a street's level of noise pollution to its house prices. Drawing these two themes together on one map allows planners to assess the impact of noise pollution. This could help them decide whether to allow a noisy business like a nightclub to open in the area.

In addition to the data, software, and hardware, the final important thing needed to make the best use of a GIS is experience. GIS can be complicated, so it is important to know exactly what kind of data is being used, how to perform the analysis, and how to produce the map. As GIS become more common in daily life, more computer scientists, geographers, and cartographers will be needed.

Using a GIS

A GIS can store lots of information about the positions of features and their attributes. It can hold very detailed information about any place in the world.

THE INFORMATION IN THE GIS IS BEST THOUGHT OF AS A series of "layers." The base layer is the outline map of the area. All the other information has to be held with the same coordinate system. This includes features like rivers, roads, towns, and cities.

All this information could be plotted on a computer screen at the same time, but it is likely that this would be too detailed and probably unreadable. Instead layers of information can be switched on and off, so they can be viewed in different combinations. In this way, users of GIS can examine the relationship between different themes, such as street lighting and location of auto accidents.

Some people use a GIS approach to a question without even knowing that they are doing it. An insurance assessor, for example, may make decisions about how likely it is that floods will hit various houses in a

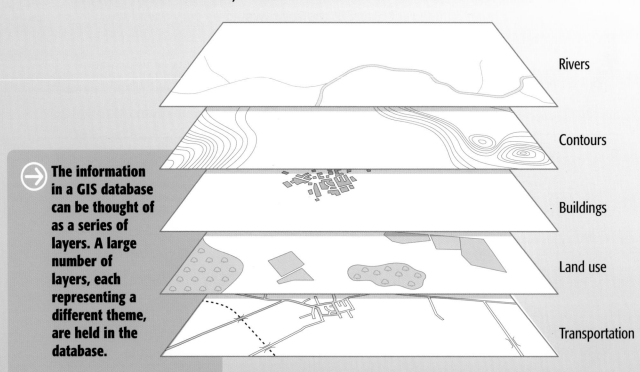

The information in a GIS database can be thought of as a series of layers. A large number of layers, each representing a different theme, are held in the database.

Rivers

Contours

Buildings

Land use

Transportation

community. In order to do this accurately, the assessor collects information such as how high above sea level each house is, how near it is to a river, how steep the slope is around the house, and what the annual rainfall is in the area. All these facts are combined to get a single percentage figure that summarizes the risk of flooding for each house. The assessor might figure out that the chance of a flood affecting a particular house in the next 10 years is two percent. A GIS would make it much easier for the assessor to carry out this task.

Route Planning

Imagine you are in charge of a command center for ambulances, fire engines, and police cars. The drivers of these vehicles rely on you to guide them by the quickest route to an emergency. The route that takes the least time is not always the shortest. A GIS could show you the maximum safe speeds on different roads and the density of traffic along them. Using this information, you would be able to figure out the quickest route to the scene of an accident. Because a GIS routing system can be updated fairly easily, it could even include information about temporary road repair work and indicate alternative roads to be followed. Geographical information systems just like this are used by emergency services in many countries, saving precious time in providing assistance.

This kind of GIS information can be bought for your own car. Many databases of national road information are available on the Internet or as part of in-car GPS systems. These databases have the digitized network of roads throughout the whole country stored on them.

A modern road traffic control center. Geographical information systems allow traffic controllers to spot patterns and predict the results of construction work or accidents in different places.

Figuring Out School Catchment Areas

Because the GIS can calculate distances easily along a road network, it can also figure out zones. The computer can make thousands of calculations much more quickly than a human being, and so, for example, can figure out the best place to build a new school. The GIS programmer inputs information about the position (street address) of all the children in a town or section of a city. Then several alternative sites are chosen for the school.

For each trial site, the total distance that all schoolchildren would need to travel is calculated by the GIS. At one site, the school might be closest for perhaps 500 children, who would travel a total of 750 miles to and from school each day. The average distance for each pupil would therefore be 1.5 miles (2.4 km) per day.

A GIS with maps, the locations of schools, and the addresses of all the children to be collected helps the planning of routes for school buses. The location of the schools themselves is also sometimes selected using GIS databases. Such databases do not include just the addresses of schoolchildren, but also records of births to plan future school building.

Cleaning up after an oil spill is expensive and time-consuming. A GIS can help monitor the movement of the oil slick and calculate how much would come ashore if the booms around the leaking ship failed. The GIS would include information about relevant local tides and currents.

At another site, closer to an existing school, the new school could be the nearest one for only 300 children. The GIS might calculate the total distance of travel per day to be 300 miles (483 km). This would be a more attractive site from the point of view of the children because each pupil would travel only 1 mile (1.6 km) per day. Planners would need to take into account that it is normally more expensive to educate a child at a smaller school than a larger one.

GIS for the Environment

GIS is also used in the natural environment to help with management tasks. For a forest manager, for example, it is useful to keep a record of the types of trees and their ages in his or her area. This can be done with a paper map, so long as it is revised every year. With a GIS, the forest manager can also plan which areas of forest should be felled next and how much timber will be produced. The manager will have a record of which parts of the forest are best suited to different species of tree and know where best to build a forest-fire observation tower. The GIS will also record vital wildlife habitats for rare types of bird.

Weather forecasts rely on GIS to help store data and predict future climate patterns. Some scientists even use GIS to try to predict floods, volcanic eruptions, and landslides.

Storing Data in a GIS

Computer programmers can store digitized data in a special way. Instead of defining points, lines, and areas as coordinates, they use small cells.

COORDINATES CAN BE HELD IN A COMPUTER AS VECTOR data. Vector data is a set of feature coordinates with some extra information about the feature, such as its name or color. Alternately, every point on the map can be given a cell, whether there is a feature there or not. If there is a feature, the cell can be switched on; if there isn't, the cell is switched off.

If the cells are very small, you cannot detect them with the naked eye. This technique is used in television, where the

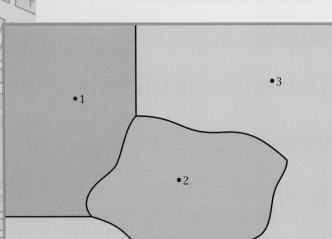

1 Residential
2 Water
3 Farmland

1	1	1	3	3	3	3	3	3
1	1	1	3	3	3	3	3	3
1	1	2	2	2	2	3	3	3
1	1	2	2	2	2	2	3	3
1	2	2	2	2	2	3	3	3
3	3	3	2	2	2	3	3	3
3	3	3	3	2	3	3	3	3
3	3	3	3	3	3	3	3	3

⬆ **Maps and the features on them are made up of points, lines, and areas. In a computer, they can be held as "vector" information and are stored as a set of coordinates.**

⬆ **To show the same map on a screen, it is held as a set of small cells called pixels. They are given a number corresponding to their color. Here the number 1 represents housing (gray), 2 is the lake (blue), and 3 is farmland (green).**

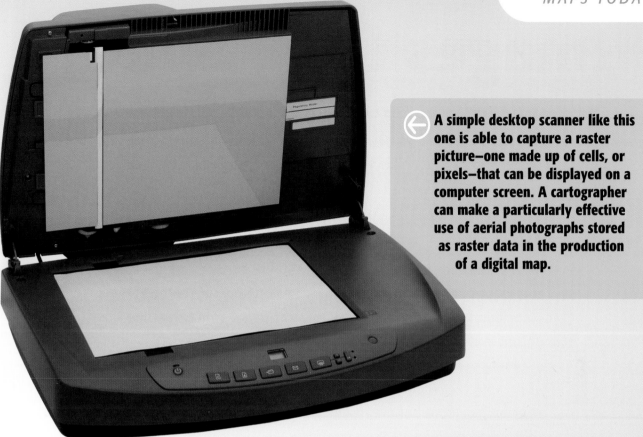

A simple desktop scanner like this one is able to capture a raster picture—one made up of cells, or pixels—that can be displayed on a computer screen. A cartographer can make a particularly effective use of aerial photographs stored as raster data in the production of a digital map.

picture on the screen is made up of thousands of small cells, called "picture elements" or "pixels" for short. Each pixel is given a color.

The same principle can be applied to a map. If a pixel covers an area where there is a lake, it can be given the color blue; if the pixel covers a line that defines a railroad, it can be black. In places where there are no features, the pixels are stored with a code or color indicating that they are only the "background" area.

A map that is stored on a computer in this way is known as a bitmap image. This data is different from vector data—it is called raster data.

Using Bitmap Images in a GIS

Some GIS are able to handle both raster data and vector data together. An aerial photograph of the area is displayed as a raster image, made up of color-coded pixels. Vector data is drawn on top of the raster layer. In the area that would be "background" on many paper maps, the raster image data shows through. It can show the gradual variation in the vegetation, agriculture, and even in the appearance of urban areas over extensive parts of the map. This means that every part of the map has some information to show.

Images from Space

Large-scale maps of Earth's surface were once produced using photographs taken from an airplane, but today orbital satellites can provide the images.

INSTEAD OF PROVIDING PHOTOGRAPHS ON FILM, MODERN equipment produces digital photographs that are already in a bitmap form suitable for handling in a computer. These images are cheaper to produce, can be wirelessly transmitted, and images can be automatically inserted into digital maps as they become available. They do not even have to be created by visible light.

Existing aerial photographs can be converted into bitmap images using a piece of equipment called a scanner. With professional-quality scanners, each pixel of the resulting bitmap image can represent an area of the original photograph as small as a $\frac{1}{6,300}$-inch square. The smaller the area that each pixel records, the higher the quality of the resulting image. This technique is limited by the quality of the original photograph.

The quality, or resolution, of bitmap images is measured by their size in pixels. A professional quality scan of a film negative, for example, will create an image that has around 9,000 pixels horizontally and 6,000 pixels vertically. The resolution of the bitmap images produced by the digital cameras in satellites and planes, on the other hand, is practically unlimited.

The actual physical size of these images depends on how small a printer or monitor can display each pixel. If a pixel is printed as a $\frac{1}{600}$-inch square, for example, then a professional quality scan of a film negative will be printed as an image 15 inches (38 cm) wide and 10 inches (25 cm) high. Increasing the size of each pixel will increase the physical size of the image, but reduce its quality.

Image Processing

Once an image is in pixel form, it can be stored in a computer or on a disk. It can also be adjusted using computer software programs called "image-processing packages." An image-processing package can stretch

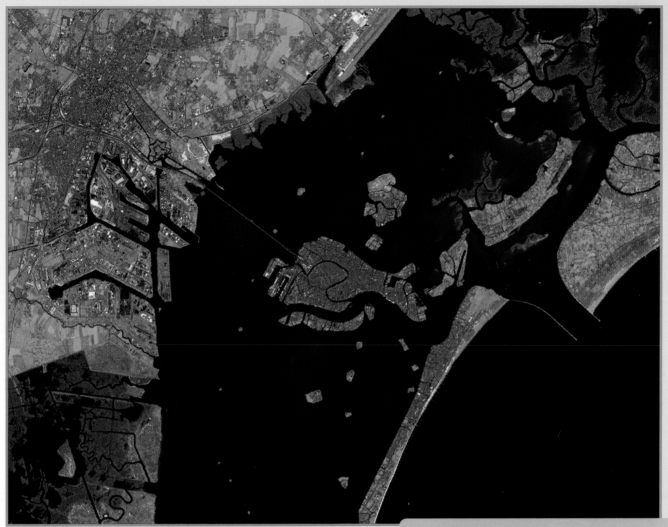

and distort raster data to make it match up to the rest of
the data in a GIS. Satellite images may not have been taken
looking straight down onto the part of Earth being
mapped, but at an angle. A map shows a straight-down
view, so if the image and the map are to be combined, the
image has to be adjusted to fit the map. This process is
called "registration" or "warping." Registration gives the
image coordinates. These can be read using the software in
the same way that the grid on a map is read.

   One of the main reasons for using image-processing software is to
detect details that the human eye finds difficult to pick out. The
software can, for example, find all the straight lines on an image. So a
satellite image can be used to pick out all the roads in an area. It is also

This picture of Venice, Italy, was
taken by a camera on board an
orbiting satellite. It is a raster
image made up of pixels that have a
resolution of one meter on the
ground. This means that it is
possible to see very small features
such as the boats in the canals, even
in an image taken from 425 miles
(680 km) above the Earth.

Extent of the Electromagnetic Spectrum

The light that we see every day from the sun or a light bulb takes up just a small part of the electromagnetic spectrum. Features on Earth reflect electromagnetic waves at different places on the spectrum in different ways, so that new ways of mapping Earth become possible. Even deep space has its own spectral signature. Gamma rays, X-rays, and radio waves detected on Earth arriving from space are the clues astronomers use in their continuing attempts to map the universe.

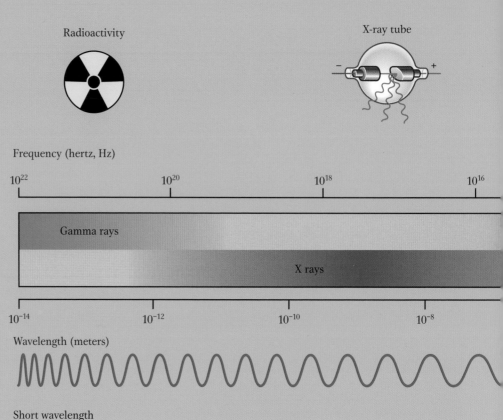

Radioactivity

X-ray tube

Frequency (hertz, Hz)

10^{22} 10^{20} 10^{18} 10^{16}

Gamma rays

X rays

10^{-14} 10^{-12} 10^{-10} 10^{-8}

Wavelength (meters)

Short wavelength

easy for the software to select all areas that look the same. A computer operator could pick out a group of pixels that are known to be forest and ask the software to find and highlight every other area with the same pattern of colors. The result is a forest map. The image-processing package can then count up the number of forest pixels and estimate the total area of forest.

Seeing Beyond Visible Light

The pictures taken using a camera in an airplane will normally show part of Earth as it is seen in the daylight. The digital sensors used are sensitive to visible light. This light comes from the sun and is reflected from features on Earth's surface. The sun's light reflects as a green color from leaves and grass, but reflects as a brown or tan color from sand and desert.

Visible light is a form of radiation. These visible light waves are part of a wide range of waves called the "spectrum." Radio waves, ultraviolet

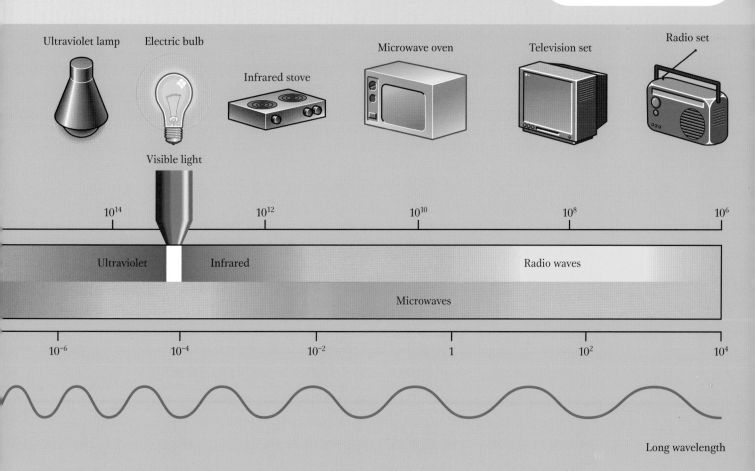

Ultraviolet lamp   Electric bulb

Infrared stove

Microwave oven   Television set   Radio set

Visible light

10^{14} 10^{12} 10^{10} 10^8 10^6

Ultraviolet   Infrared   Radio waves

Microwaves

10^{-6} 10^{-4} 10^{-2} 1 10^2 10^4

Long wavelength

rays, infrared light, and X-rays are also part of the spectrum. Images from different parts of the spectrum provide different information. For example, infrared radiation images highlight water features. Infrared light is absorbed almost completely by water, so it appears black on infrared film. Infrared can also be used to show vegetation that has disease: healthy trees reflect more infrared, while dying trees absorb it.

Spectral Signatures

Environmental scientists have noticed that many features on Earth's surface reflect different parts of the spectrum in different ways. This pattern of reflectance is called the spectral signature. The spectral signature of rocks with high iron content, for example, differs from rocks with a high aluminum content.

The imaging equipment on board satellites is able to sense reflectance in many different parts of the spectrum. This helps in mapping rock types, soil classification, vegetation species, and other natural features.

The images can also pick up man-made features. Roads, for example, reflect radiation in a different way than gardens.

Many satellite missions are launched with spectral imaging equipment designed to identify specific features. Some satellites look at weather patterns on Earth's surface; others map currents and waves. Some missions examine the growth of deserts; others show how cities are expanding across the world.

Advantages of Satellite Data

If we want to use satellite images to create maps of desert growth or urban expansion, we can capture data from more than one moment in time. Then we can create a map showing the difference between the earlier size of the desert or city and the up-to-date one. Using satellite images of the same area of Earth taken at different times, we can examine the effect of global warming. The technology enables researchers to track large-scale changes like the melting of the ice at the North and South poles.

Because the cameras are on unmanned satellites and can last up to 20 years, they are a relatively inexpensive way of obtaining images of Earth's surface for mapping and environmental monitoring.

Producing images from different parts of the

→ **Reflectance across the visible part of the spectrum for Africa, from images taken by the Landsat Thematic Mapper satellite.**

➜ Deforestation is clearly shown in this Landsat view of Rondonia, Brazil. The jungle, shown in red, is being cleared on a huge scale by farmers burning the trees (blue areas).

spectrum means that satellite scanners can detect and map many different types of features. All the images sent back from satellites to Earth are already in digital raster form. So we can include the images in geographical information systems for visual display. In addition, the data can be processed using image-processing software packages, and extra information can be obtained from it.

Resolution of Satellite Images

One of the major problems with satellite data is its resolution. Because satellites orbit high above Earth's surface, the area represented by each pixel of a satellite image is usually quite large. This means that the images cannot be used to identify small features. However, there are spy satellites that carry precision telescopes looking down at Earth. Such satellites produce high-resolution images that can even show people.

The images beaming back to Earth from commercial mapping satellites are not as high-resolution as spy satellite images. When the first Landsat mission went into orbit in 1972, each pixel of the images sent back represented an area of about 67,000 square feet (6,200 sq m) on the ground. Later missions have provided images with much higher resolution. Today pictures from space can be as detailed as pictures taken from airplanes.

The Stars and Planets

All the features we see on maps are located on the surface of a globe, our Earth. The other bodies in our solar system can be mapped in the same way.

WE CAN MAP OTHER PLANETS IN OUR SOLAR system just as we have mapped Earth if we can record their surfaces. But how do we map the positions of the stars in space? There is no "surface" to map.

The environments of other planetary bodies are very different from Earth, so it is difficult to use exactly the same mapping techniques. Without sea, there is no concept of sea level, so how do we measure the heights of mountains on Mars? The answer is to take the lowest point we can find and the highest mountain, then layer tint the map accordingly. How can we get images of

This color-coded map of Mars uses the same techniques as Earth mapping to display the height of the mountains on the "red planet." Millions of heights were obtained from an altimeter (height-measuring instrument) orbiting Mars. The large mountain to the upper right of this image is Olympus Mons, the largest volcano in our solar system.

Utopia Planitia

Olympus Mons

Chryse Planitia

Isidis Planitia

Elysium Mons

Amazonis Planitia

Meridiani Planum

Tharsis Montes

Valles Marineris

Gusev Crater

Argyre Planitia

Hellas Planitia

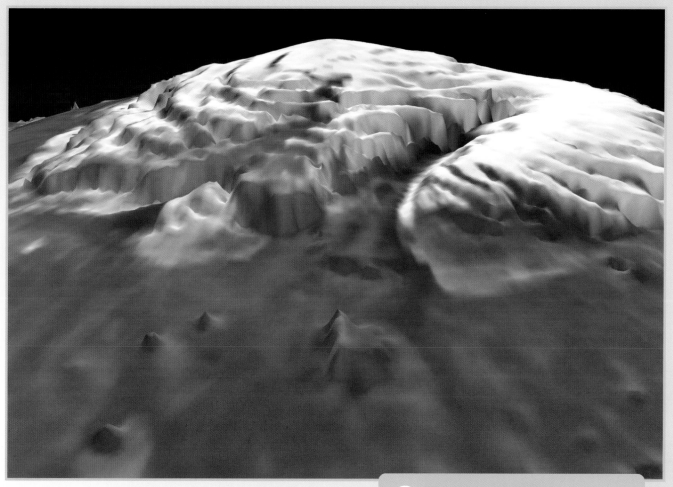

This three-dimensional topographical projection shows the north pole of the planet Mars. It was created in 1999 using around 2.6 million laser-pulse measurements of the terrain made by the Mars Global Surveyor satellite.

the surface of Venus when it is always covered with clouds? Satellite radar is one technique.

If the planet or moon is not a true sphere, which is true for most of Jupiter's moons, how can we use map projections to create a flat paper map? We compromise: after all, Earth is not a true sphere either.

Telescopes have been used in the past to examine the moon, Venus, and Mars, our closest heavenly bodies (although telescopes are useless for seeing through the thick clouds around Venus). For planetary mapping beyond these three heavenly bodies, techniques rely on satellite-based images sent back as digital raster pictures to Earth. They are collected using radar, television cameras, and other imaging equipment.

Mapping the Night Sky

When we look at ways of mapping outer space, we come across a range of difficulties. The universe is not a flat or a familiar globe shape, so it is tricky to come up with a method for locating features. Coordinates cannot be used in the same way as they are on the surface of Earth. In the vastness of the universe, what should we use as a "zero point" from which all measurements will be taken? The objects in the universe that we may want to

This three-dimensional view of a 3-mile (5-km) high volcano on the surface of Venus is a combination of radar images and altimeter data. Venus is covered with cloud, and is never as clear as this; the image has been colored to highlight lava flows.

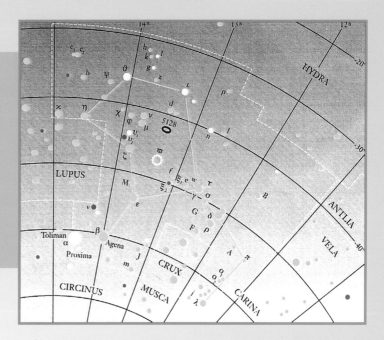

This is part of a map of the "celestial globe." Instead of latitude and longitude, declination (–40°, –30°, and –20°) and right ascension (measured in hours, 12, 13, and 14) are shown. This section of the sky contains the Centaurus constellation. Just like a terrestrial map, some features—certain stars— are considered important enough to be named; others are not.

measure and plot, and perhaps use as zero points of reference, such as galaxies and black holes, are either too large and three-dimensional or else cannot be sensed accurately enough because they are not light enough or are too far away.

The main solution to the problem of mapping of the sky is to imagine a large globe with Earth at its center. It is called the celestial globe. The locations of all the visible comets, planets, stars, and galaxies can be plotted on the inside of that globe. The distance of these objects away from Earth is ignored. All that is recorded is their position as they appear from Earth. Even though the objects are plotted on the inside of the globe (rather than the outside, which is what is done when maps are made of Earth), we can still create a reference system, like latitude and longitude, to locate them.

The system is very similar to Earth's location system. There are "celestial poles," which are the points on the celestial globe directly above Earth's poles. There is a "celestial equator" drawn around the celestial globe above Earth's equator. Instead of using latitude and longitude to position features on the inside of the celestial globe, the terms used are "declination" and "right ascension."

The major problem is that the position of stars and planets in the sky is constantly changing. Every map of the night sky has to indicate the time of day and the day of the year at which it is a true picture.

Modern Maps

We can only be absolutely sure what is under the earth by tunneling, mining, and digging. Modern instruments can give us useful clues without all the hard work.

GEOLOGISTS HAVE BEEN MAKING MAPS OF THE ROCK beneath our feet over the last two centuries. This has been done in order to find and mine the rich resources of Earth, such as coal, gold, and oil.

The earliest geologists interpreted rock layers by looking at the shape of the surface of Earth. Later methods involved scientific examination of soil samples and trial drilling. Following the invention of the airplane, exploration geologists used air photographs both to make maps and to interpret the patterns of Earth's surface. They looked for large geological structures, such as fault lines and rock basins, which might not be obvious from ground level.

Sometimes it is possible to predict the existence of certain minerals in the ground by looking at the vegetation shown on the photographs. Some species of tree, for example, grow faster and healthier on soil with a high

This is a satellite radar "contour map" of the results of a California earthquake. By combining the "before" and "after" images, each color band shows a 4-inch (10-cm) movement in Earth's surface.

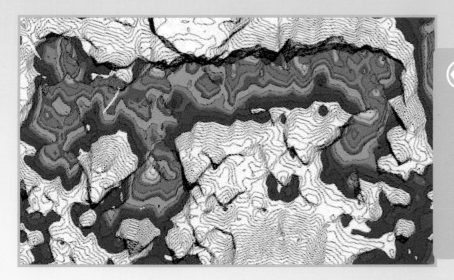

This is a magnetic map of a burial mound. Created in A.D. 600, the bear-shaped mound is at the Effigy Mounds National Monument, Iowa. The disturbance of the ground and the creation of the mound by native tribes have led to variation in the magnetic properties below the surface.

concentration of manganese than on soil containing a large amount of some other minerals (such as aluminum).

A magnetometer can also be used from an airplane. It is sensitive to magnetic variation in Earth's surface and can be used to find iron ore and other magnetic minerals.

Satellite images can also be used in exploration for minerals. The spectral signature of different minerals (see page 23) can reveal outcrops of valuable resources. Image-processing techniques can be used to detect and zoom into likely areas of mineral wealth.

Ground-Penetrating Radar

Ground-penetrating radar allows images to be captured of solid objects buried about 10 feet (3 m) below the surface. Once a site has been cleared of vegetation and other surface features, a transmitting antenna is placed on, or into, the ground. A radio signal sent into the ground reflects in different ways from different materials. The soil conducts the signal better or worse depending on its type and the amount of moisture in it. The most obvious features picked up are boundaries between soil and metal, and disturbed or undisturbed ground.

Archaeologists use ground-penetrating radar to detect burial sites, ancient roadways, and outlines of buildings before undertaking archaeological digs. Maintenance engineers find underground radar maps useful for finding wires and pipes. Accurate radar information helps keep roadwork and disruption to a minimum.

Microscopic Mapping

Most maps show large areas, such as your neighborhood or even a whole country. The scale can also be reversed, and things smaller than the map can be the subject.

SCIENTISTS USE THE TECHNIQUES OF LANDSCAPE MAPPING to map microscopic surfaces, such as bits of metal and computer chips. Contours show the shape of all the small depressions and the rough surface. Minute cracks can also be detected. Such maps are used for quality control in precision engineering.

Mapping the Human Genome

Modeling of molecules—showing how atoms combine with each other—is a kind of three-dimensional mapping. This kind of mapping is being used to record the human genome. The genome is the combined "set of instructions," or "blueprint," that is in the nucleus of every cell in the human body. The human genome is made up of at least 30,000 genes (some say 80,000). These genes together tell cells how to split to reproduce themselves, organize, and come together to create a human being.

This is a computer-generated view of DNA. The blue nitrogen, the yellow carbon and phosphorus, and the red oxygen atoms are joined by cross-linked nucleotide bases. This is not a photograph of DNA: it is a visual representation that can be read like a map.

Like maps of the world, maps of the genome are made at different scales. The largest scale map shows DNA and its components. A smaller-scale map represents the way in which the genes together build up into chromosomes, of which each cell nucleus has 46. Chromosomes are relatively large. They are made up of 3 billion DNA base pairs! Using high-magnification electron microscopes, geneticists can map the location of the DNA threads along the chromosomes.

Creating the Map

The ultimate aim is to create a map of the whole human genome. It is the complete DNA sequence for the whole of each chromosome. This is a very complex set of molecules to display, and digital cartographic methods are one of the tools helping us picture the building blocks of human life.

The sequence of DNA patterns can be coded and brought together into a map of the whole human genome. This plot of the elements of one gene shows all of the DNA sequences. It is being digitized.

Visualization

Maps are really good tools for "visualizing" Earth. They simplify the picture of the real world. Maps can also give a clearer explanation than a list of statistics.

ANY LIST OF CONNECTED NUMBERS IS MUCH BETTER shown as a picture of some kind. A set of temperatures over a month or year, the value of shares on the stock exchange, or the population density of a number of countries can be plotted onto a graph. The conversion of numbers, facts, and positions into graphs, charts, and maps is called "visualization."

Today scientists and other people have to store and handle increasing quantities of information. Scientific experiments can produce huge amounts of data and statistics, far more than scientists could have gathered together before computers.

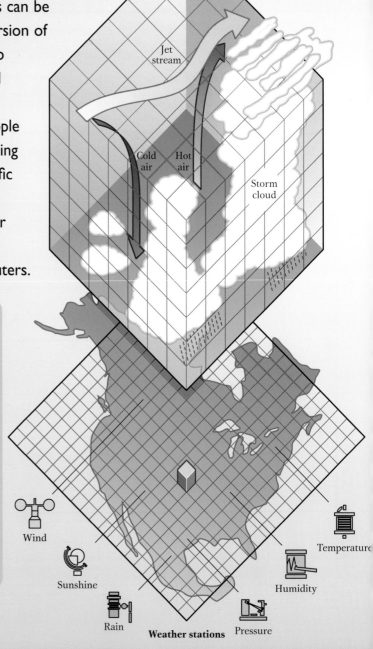

Jet stream

Cold air

Hot air

Storm cloud

Wind

Sunshine

Rain

Weather stations

Pressure

Humidity

Temperature

Many different weather observations by different instruments provide the data for this model of the weather in part of the atmosphere over the Midwest. The three-dimensional diagram is a good summary of the weather conditions. If further observations were added (for the days before and after), a "movie" could be created in a computer showing changes over a period of time. The computer can analyze the patterns to predict the coming weather.

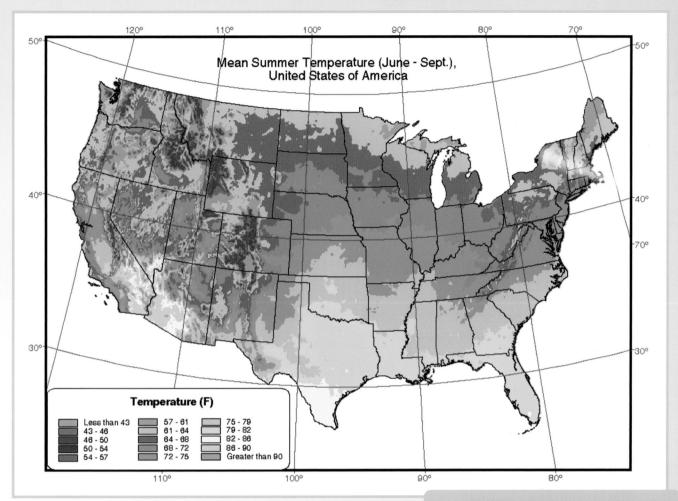

**Mean Summer Temperature (June - Sept.),
United States of America**

Temperature (F)

Less than 43	57 - 61	75 - 79
43 - 46	61 - 64	79 - 82
46 - 50	64 - 68	82 - 86
50 - 54	68 - 72	86 - 90
54 - 57	72 - 75	Greater than 90

This map summarizes a large amount of data that, if presented only as a list of statistics, would be very difficult to understand. The average summer temperature across the United States is mapped by the Spatial Climate Analysis Service, Oregon State University.

Meteorologists, for example, record thousands of daily readings of temperature, humidity, and pressure. Some scientists rely on equipment that is not operated by a human being but is switched on and sends back information to their office all the time. There are instruments placed on the sides of volcanoes and at potential earthquake sites to check ground movement 24 hours a day. Mapping scientists also use unmanned instruments sending back information. The remote sensing satellites are constantly beaming back thousands of raster images.

All this information needs to be recorded and analyzed, and one of the best ways of bringing it together and making some sense of it is to visualize it. When the information is about Earth or about people spread over a large area like a city or nation, a map is the best visualization tool.

Virtual Environments

Modern computer technology has enabled the creation of three-dimensional, realistic depictions of the real world. These can be used for entertainment or practical purposes.

In medieval Europe, cartographers frequently produced "maps" of fantastical islands, continents, and even the afterlife. As maps of the real world became more detailed, so too did the maps of these imaginary places. Modern computer technology has allowed the creation of highly detailed and immersive virtual worlds. As with cartographic advances of the past, this new technology has been used to depict both real and imaginary places.

The most prominent use of these virtual worlds is in the field of computer games. The virtual environments of games are often representations of real places, created using the same techniques as cartography. Modern racing games, for example, often feature accurate reproductions of real-world racetracks. In order to create these virtual tracks, the real ones have to be surveyed in painstaking detail. Every drop or rise in the track is carefully recorded, and the precise shape of each corner is mapped. Some games reproduce tracks so accurately that real racing drivers use them for practice!

This shows the interior of a cockpit flight simulator for the Boeing 737-300 airliner. The to-scale view of the landscape outside is computer-generated.

→ These soldiers are using the *America's Army* computer game. The current version of the game is used primarily to give potential recruits an idea of what combat is like. However, some studies have suggested that it could be used to train soldiers.

The principles of cartography are also important to the creation of imaginary landscapes. When designing a virtual city, for example, developers will spend months examining maps of real cities. This research helps them create a believable virtual city, with homes, businesses, and industries laid out in realistic patterns. Similarly, by studying topographic maps, developers can isolate recurring patterns and rules that describe the shape of different landscapes. These rules can then be used to make programs that generate believable, imaginary landscapes for games.

Not Just for Entertainment

In addition to being an important part of computer games, virtual environments are also used for serious practical applications. Simulators, for example, are an essential part of the training of airplane pilots. These simulators use accurate maps as the basis for their virtual landscapes. This means they can even be used to teach visual navigation or to practice landing approaches to real world airports. As virtual worlds become more detailed, the number of practical applications will increase. They are already being considered for use in training soldiers, for example, and are widely used by researchers and journalists.

The most widely used application of this new technology, however, is the creation of new types of maps. Maps based on three-dimensional virtual globes, such as Google Earth, present the user with a map that does not need any prior knowledge to interpret. A user can look at maps, satellite photographs, or even panoramic pictures taken at street level, and plan a route using visible landmarks.

Online Mapping

The most important method of communicating information today is the Internet, the huge network of computers and connections that spans the world.

THE INTERNET HAS REVOLUTIONIZED THE WAY THAT MAPS are presented and used. Early online maps were essentially just scans of existing paper maps. The user could scroll across the area covered, and perhaps zoom in or out, but could not interact with the map in any way.

The first major advance was the use of fully digitized maps. Unlike the scanned maps that came before them, these maps were created using vector graphics (see page 19). They could be zoomed in and out to a far greater extent than raster images, and the level of detail displayed could be programmed to increase and decrease as the user zoomed in or out. These digital maps could also be easily and frequently updated—individual sections of the map could be changed without having to redraw or replace the rest of the map.

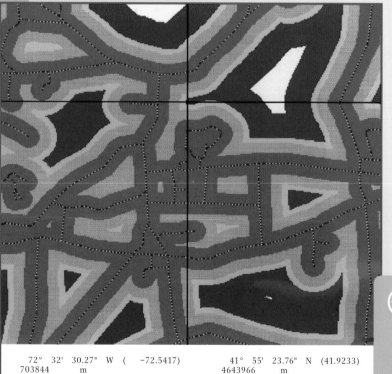

```
   72° 32' 30.27" W  (  -72.5417)        41° 55' 23.76" N  (41.9233)
   703844      m                       4643966       m
   9723        univ                    5434          univ
   Grid Reference      18TYB  384443966

well  PROXIMITY TO WELLS                .5    km
circ  PROXIMITY TO POLLUTION            1     km
road  CORRIDORS FROM ROADS              .5    km
slop  COMPOSITE SLOPE                   0     %
```

Scientists and researchers can also get access to mapping information quickly and easily. This map is part of a GIS database that analyzes the risks of pollution of the water supply. The map reader can position the "crosshair" pointer–the two dark lines–anywhere on the map and obtain a readout of latitude, longitude, distance from wells, and other information.

The following text appears on the device screen:

A302 Saint Margaret Street (70/71)   15:11

Little Sanctuary
Parliament Square

Parliament Street

Canon Row

650 m   Hotovo

Most online mapping services now use maps that display a combination of raster and vector data. The vector maps representing streets, rivers, and important buildings are overlaid on satellite and aerial photographs. This allows the important practical features of the map to be clearly visible and labeled, while providing an overview of the landscape at the same time.

This in-car map is continually updated through a mobile phone connection to the Internet. The map face changes as the driver moves toward the edge of the mapped area, recentering the display and zooming into the fine detail if necessary.

User-Submitted Information

The most recent innovation is the linking of maps to other online resources. A map of New York, for example, could contain thousands of icons that link places on the map to relevant websites. An icon over a restaurant might link you to a review, or an icon over a waterfront museum might link to a collection of historic photos. These links do not have to be added by the cartographer; they can be added by users with knowledge of the area. This process allows maps to display places in more detail than could be managed by even a massive team of professional researchers.

Glossary

Words in *italics* have their own entries in the glossary.

aerial photograph (or air photograph) – a photograph looking straight down at Earth

altimeter – on Earth, an instrument that measures height above sea level, usually put in an aircraft; in space, an instrument that can record the height of points on a planet's surface above or below a selected zero position

archaeology – the science of interpreting the past by examining remains, usually dug up from underground

astronomer – one who studies celestial bodies (planets and stars) and the universe as a whole

attribute – a particular characteristic of an object or feature shown on a map, such as the pollution in a lake or the name of a building

black hole – an object in the universe that is so dense and large that its immensely strong gravity even sucks in radiation such as light. Because of this, black holes cannot be seen, but they can be located by the complete lack of radiation.

cartography – the task of collecting information and producing maps. People who do this are called cartographers.

catchment area – the area from which people are allocated to a particular school, hospital, or other public body

celestial globe – a model of the imaginary sphere enclosing the universe, with Earth at the center, that maps the relative position of the planets, stars, and *constellations* as they appear to us in the skies

chromosomes – the rod-shaped structures in a cell nucleus made up of the genes that pass on characteristics from one generation to the next. The number of chromosomes is the same in every cell, but varies from one species of plant or animal to the next.

An aerial photograph of the crowds gathered for the inauguration of President Barack Obama in January 2009. This picture was taken from an aircraft flying below cloud-level for a better view.

The constellations appear to us as closely grouped patterns of stars. In reality they are made from stars and galaxies that are often millions of light-years apart. The Andromeda galaxy, for example, is over 2 million light-years further away than the other objects in its constellation.

computer graphics – how graphical features, such as maps, are displayed and manipulated on the screen of a computer

constellation – a group of fixed stars in the night sky appearing to form a group. Usually named with reference to the shape the group takes, for example, the Big Dipper.

contour – an imaginary line connecting places in the landscape that are at equal height above (or below) sea level. The distance of contour lines from each other on a map shows how steeply or gradually land rises.

coordinates – the pair of values that define a position on a graph or on a map with a coordinate system (such as latitude and longitude). On a map, the coordinates "55°N 45°E" indicate a position of 55 degrees north of latitude, 45 degrees east of longitude.

database – a collection of facts, measurements, or information stored in a digital form

declination – the angular distance of an astronomical body measured in degrees from the celestial equator along the great circle passing through it and the celestial poles

diesel – a thick oily fuel that is obtained from the distilling of petroleum. Some cars and trains are powered by diesel-powered engines.

digitizing – the task of converting information and images, such as maps, into the form of numbers that can be stored in a computer

DNA (deoxyribonucleic acid) – an extremely long molecule that is the main component of *chromosomes* and is the material that transfers genetic characteristics in all life

equator – an imaginary line running around Earth at equal distance from the North and South Poles. It is the line at 0 degrees *latitude*.

geographic information system (GIS) – a computer-based digital store of geographic information about an area, which can be consulted and analyzed

41

geology – the study of the rocks under Earth's surface and their structure

Global Positioning System (GPS) – a system of 24 satellites orbiting Earth and sending out highly accurate radio signals indicating where they are. A GPS receiver held by someone on Earth can interpret the signals and calculate the receiver's position on Earth.

human genome – the full set of *chromosomes* that together define all the characteristics that human beings inherit from their parents

icon – a small image on a computer screen that represents something, for example, a program or device that is activated by a mouse click; or any picture or symbol universally recognized to represent something

image processing – the modification of photographs or satellite images by computer software

infrared – a part of the *spectrum* close to red. Infrared radiation is not visible to the eye but can be recorded by some sensors

Internet – the network of interconnected computers throughout the world linked by wires and satellites and running software to allow them to communicate with each other

latitude – the line joining places of equal angular distance from the center of Earth in a north-south direction. The equator is 0 degrees latitude, the poles are at 90 degrees latitude north and south.

layer tinting – showing height of mountains and hills on a map using bands of color to define zones where the land is between two height measurements (between 100 and 250 meters above sea level, for example)

Until the invention of ground-penetrating radar and seismic surveying equiment, the only way to study the geology of an area was to find places where erosion had exposed the underlying rock.

longitude – a line connecting places of equal angular distance from the center of Earth, measured in degrees east or west of the Prime Meridian, which is at 0 degrees longitude

magnetometer – an instrument held manually or mounted on or suspended from an airplane to measure the strength and direction of Earth's magnetic field

meteorologist – a person who studies and records the weather, often using and producing maps. Meteorologists also make weather forecasts.

nucleotide bases – nucleotides are the chemical compounds that make up a *DNA* molecule. Each nucleotide consists of three units: deoxyribose (a sugar molecule), a phosphate group, and one of four different nitrogen-containing compounds called bases.

orbital – belonging to or relating to a path around a celestial body such as a planet, moon, or satellite

outcrop – a projection from the surface

phenomena – a fact or occurrence, ordinary or extraordinary, that can be observed

pixel – short for "picture element"; the small "building block" of a *raster* image. Raster images consist entirely of regularly shaped small pixels, which, when viewed together, give the impression of a continuous image. Each pixel presents one shade or color in the image.

raster data – image data made up of *pixels* plus associated information

reflectance – a measure of the ability of a surface to reflect light or other radiation

registration – the task of ensuring that map data sets correspond with each other and can be overlaid, checking that the data layers have the same *coordinate* system and projection. Similarly, when an image is printed, the *pixels* on the separate pieces of color film can be "out of register" if the films are not placed exactly on top of each other.

relevant – having some bearing on or importance to an issue

relief – the shape of Earth's surface, especially its hills, mountains, and depressions

remote sensing – the taking of digital pictures of Earth from orbiting satellites

resolution – the size of the *pixels* in a *raster* image relative to the true size of the object recorded. A satellite image showing pixels equivalent to 1,000 meters on Earth is a low-resolution image compared to an image with a 10-meter pixel resolution.

right ascension – one of the two reference points in the equatorial coordinate system for specifying the position of an astronomical object on the celestial sphere

scanning – sweeping across an image or part of Earth's surface with a device that can sense and record variation in the light

sensors – a device capable of detecting and responding to physical stimuli such as movement, light, or heat

software – computer programs that run the operation of computer hardware (parts of the computer)

spectral signatures – the characteristic shape of the curve on a graph showing *reflectance* of an object of different parts of the *spectrum*

Modern flight simulators use exact copies of the cockpits of real aircraft in addition to highly detailed virtual environments that model phenomena as complex as weather conditions and turbulence.

spectrum – the electromagnetic spectrum comprises the radiation of the colors of light visible to the human eye along with all other invisible waves emitted, such as X-rays and ultraviolet light

surveying – the measuring of altitudes, angles, and distances on the land surface in order to obtain accurate positions of features that can be mapped. Surveying the oceans and seas also means measuring distances and angles between visible coastal positions, but the third dimension measured is depth rather than height.

three-dimensional – possessing or appearing to possess the dimensions of height, width, and depth

topographic map – a map that shows natural features, such as hills, rivers, and forests, and man-made features, such as roads and buildings

vector data – digital data made up of a set of *coordinates* plus associated information. Mapping vector data is a digital record of points, lines, and areas held in a database.

vegetation – plants in general or the mass of plants growing in a particular place

virtual environment – artificially created computerized data that, with the correct software, creates the impression of the real world. The best example is the virtual training cockpit of an airplane used in flight simulation.

warping – a form of *registration*; distorting an image to make it fit the *coordinate* system of another data set

Further Reading and Web Sites

Aczel, Amir D. *The Riddle of the Compass: The Invention That Changed the World*. New York: Harcourt, 2001.

Arnold, Caroline. *The Geography Book: Activities for Exploring, Mapping, and Enjoying Your World*. New York: Wiley, 2002.

Barber, Peter, and April Carlucci, eds. *The Lie of the Land*. London: British Library Publications, 2001.

Brown, Carron, ed. *The Best-Ever Book of Exploration*. New York: Kingfisher Books, 2002.

Davis, Graham. *Make Your Own Maps*. New York: Sterling, 2008.

Deboo, Ana. *Mapping the Seas and Skies*. Chicago: Heinemann-Raintree, 2007.

Dickinson, Rachel. *Tools of Navigation: A Kid's Guide to the History & Science of Finding Your Way*. White River Junction, VT: Nomad Press, 2005.

Doak, Robin S. *Christopher Columbus: Explorer of the New World*. Minneapolis, MN: Compass Point Books, 2005.

Ehrenberg, Ralph E. *Mapping the World: An Illustrated History of Cartography*. Washington, D.C.: National Geographic, 2005.

Field, Paula, ed. *The Kingfisher Student Atlas of North America*. Boston: Kingfisher, 2005.

Ganeri, Anita, and Andrea Mills. *Atlas of Exploration*. New York: DK Publishing, 2008.

Graham, Alma, ed. *Discovering Maps*. Maplewood, NJ: Hammond World Atlas Corporation, 2004.

Harvey, Miles. *The Island of Lost Maps: A True Story of Cartographic Crime*. New York: Random House, 2000.

Harwood, Jeremy. *To the Ends of the Earth: 100 Maps That Changed the World*. Newton Abbot, United Kingdom: David and Charles, 2006.

Haywood, John. *Atlas of World History*. New York: Barnes and Noble, 1997.

Hazen, Walter A. *Everyday Life: Exploration & Discovery*. Tuscon, AZ: Good Year Books, 2005.

Henzel, Cynthia Kennedy. *Mapping History*. Edina, MN: Abdo Publishing, 2008.

Jacobs, Frank. *Strange Maps: An Atlas of Cartographic Curiosities*. New York: Viking Studio, 2009.

Keay, John. *The Great Arc: The Dramatic Tale of How India Was Mapped and Everest Was Named*. New York: Harper Collins, 2000.

Levy, Janey. *Mapping America's Westward Expansion: Applying Geographic Tools And Interpreting Maps*. New York: Rosen Publishing, 2005.

Levy, Janey. *The Silk Road: Using a Map Scale to Measure Distances*. New York: PowerKids Press, 2005.

McDonnell, Mark D. *Maps on File*. New York: Facts on File, 2007.

McNeese, Tim. *Christopher Columbus and the Discovery of the Americas*. Philadelphia: Chelsea House, 2006.

Mitchell, Robert, and Donald Prickel. *Contemporary's Number Power: Graphs, Tables, Schedules, and Maps*. Lincolnwood, IL: Contemporary Books, 2000.

Oleksy, Walter G. *Mapping the Seas*. New York: Franklin Watts, 2003.

Oleksy, Walter G. *Mapping the Skies*. New York: Franklin Watts, 2003.

Resnick, Abraham. *Maps Tell Stories Too: Geographic Connections to American History*. Bloomington, IN: IUniverse, 2002.

Rirdan, Daniel. *Wide Ranging World Map*. Phoenix, AZ: Exploration, 2002.

Ross, Val. *The Road to There: Mapmakers and Their Stories*. Toronto, Canada: Tundra Books, 2009.

Rumsey, David, and Edith M. Punt. *Cartographica Extraordinaire: The Historical Map Transformed.* Redlands, CA: Esri Press, 2004.

Short, Charles Rennie. *The World through Maps.* Buffalo, NY: Firefly Books, 2003.

Smith, A. G. *Where Am I? The Story of Maps and Navigation.* Toronto, Canada: Fitzhenry and Whiteside, 2001.

Taylor, Barbara. *Looking at Maps.* North Mankato, MN: Franklin Watts, 2007.

Taylor, Barbara. *Maps and Mapping.* New York: Kingfisher, 2002.

Virga, Vincent. *Cartographia: Mapping Civilizations.* London: Little, Brown and Company, 2007.

Wilkinson, Philip. *The World of Exploration.* New York: Kingfisher, 2006.

Wilson, Patrick. *Navigation and Signalling.* Broomall, PA: Mason Crest Publishers, 2002.

Winchester, Simon. *The Map That Changed the World: William Smith and the Birth of Modern Geology.* New York: HarperCollins, 2001.

Zuravicky, Orli. *Map Math: Learning About Latitude and Longitude Using Coordinate Systems.* New York: PowerKids Press, 2005.

Online Resources

www.davidrumsey.com
The David Rumsey map collection. This online library contains around 20,000 historical and modern maps.

http://dma.jrc.it
The mapping collection of the European Commission Joint Research Center. Includes ineractive maps as well as maps documenting environmental and human disasters around the world.

http://etc.usf.edu/Maps/
The University of South Florida's online mapping library. The collection includes historical and modern maps from around the world.

www.lib.utexas.edu/maps
The University of Texas's online map library. The collection includes old CIA maps, historical maps, and thematic maps from around the world.

www2.lib.virginia.edu/exhibits/lewis_clark
An online exhibition at the University of Virginia with information on historic expeditions, including Lewis and Clark.

http://maps.google.com
Google's online mapping resource, includes conventional maps and satellite images for most of the world, as well as street-level photography of Western urban centers.

http://maps.nationalgeographic.com
National Geographic's online mapping service.

http://memory.loc.gov/ammem/gmdhtml/
Map collections from 1500–1999 at the Library of Congress. The collection includes maps made by early explorers, maps of military campaigns, and thematic maps on a variety of topics.

www.nationalatlas.gov
Online national atlas for the United States. Includes customizable topographic maps on a range of different themes.

http://strangemaps.wordpress.com
A frequently updated collection of unusual maps, from maps of imaginary lands to creative ways of displaying data in map form.

www.unc.edu/awmc/mapsforstudents.html
A large collection of free maps, covering many different subjects and regions, hosted by the University of North Carolina.

www.un.org/Depts/Cartographic/
   english/htmain.htm
United Nations mapping agency website. contains maps of the world from 1945 to the present day, including UN maps of conflict areas and disputed territories.

Index

Page numbers written in **boldface** refer to pictures or captions.

47